AF347782

I am Who You Say I am

A guidebook for soul searching

Marjorie Tadeo Aglugub

Ukiyoto Publishing

All global publishing rights are held by

Ukiyoto Publishing

Published in 2022

Content Copyright © Marjorie Tadeo Aglugub

ISBN 9789360163778

All rights reserved.

No part of this publication may be reproduced, transmitted, or stored in a retrieval system, in any form by any means, electronic, mechanical, photocopying, recording or otherwise, without the prior permission of the publisher.

The moral rights of the author have been asserted.

This is a work of fiction. Names, characters, businesses, places, events, locales, and incidents are either the products of the author's imagination or used in a fictitious manner. Any resemblance to actual persons, living or dead, or actual events is purely coincidental.

This book is sold subject to the condition that it shall not by way of trade or otherwise, be lent, resold, hired out or otherwise circulated, without the publisher's prior consent, in any form of binding or cover other than that in which it is published.

I dedicate this book to those who are in the verge of losing their identity.

Acknowledgement

My gratitude goes to the following who helped me complete this humble masterpiece:

My coach, Sir Jonas Dupo, who paved the way to the realization of my dream to be published. His motivational words helped eliminate my doubts. He inspired me to continue writing by constantly reminding me to prioritize my passion.

My editor, Ma'am Ana Grasya whose dedication and commitment motivated me to keep going.

My fellow authors for their motivational support.

Pastor Cristopher Ayson, for all the teachings and learnings he imparted. He has helped me grow spiritually.

My very supportive parents, thank you for the love, guidance and encouragement.

My siblings, Mariel Aglugub and Caren A. Blanza who boosted my confidence. Thank you for the moral and financialsupport.

My friends, and fellow youth in the ministry who showered me with positivity.

Above all, to God who bestowed me the knowledge and wisdom. I am forever indebted.

-Marjorie

Testimonials

Randy Paderes, CPA

Lecturer/Professor/Author, (That tadhana called accounting and bakit advanced ang accounting)

The book **"I am who you say I am"** provides a realistic depiction of reality and motivates us to accomplish our objectives. Wherever we are at this moment, we are always waging a struggle inside of us that seems like a storm. We were disoriented and felt as though we had done nothing, which caused us to focus only on ourselves. Some of us experience this pressure as a result of others' successes.

Surrounding us, particularly while we are still so young, we think that after we finish our education, we will be able to support our parents, get access to the things we want, and become affluent and successful overnight. But we never know that the first five years following graduation are the times when we are still making up for the time we lost while we were studying.

Each of us is going through a distinct stage of life. Every activity has its time. We start comparing our circumstances to those of others again when anxieties hit, which makes us sad.

If this circumstance arises, we must look at our own path and never compare it to other situations. Even if we occasionally experience delays, the fact is that most of the time these delays are for the best. Yes, everyone has their own sense of time. It's important not to put ourselves under unnecessary pressure by assuming that others are far more advanced than we are. And if there is pressure, we will experience that insecurity and personal remoteness. Let's always be reminded to keep our eyes on the prize, to stay on track, and to take action to get it.

Envy over the achievements of others will only prevent us from seeing the tremendous benefits that God is pouring into our lives. Instead of always experiencing this and whining, we ought to evaluate ourselves. Are we making any efforts to fulfill our hopes and dreams? If not, we should be held accountable since we actually have the ability to obtain it. Simply said, we need to assess how much of a sacrifice we are prepared to make. And when we already have it, we shouldn't lose sight of remaining humble and not using it as an excuse to put ourselves above others and show that we are superior to them.

If we actually possess knowledge, we will never think of ourselves as superior to others. We may occasionally feel content with our lives and even brag about it, but everyone has their own preferences and choices. Others may not care how much we appreciate our successes since they may be content with their current situation and have interests unrelated to ours. This demonstrates that our happiness is what matters the most. Despite the fact that we may continue to worry a lot, what we see is only a small portion of the picture. What they will say is something we are unsure about. Everyone is always unaware of a secret tale unless they have a clear understanding of its whole context. Success cannot, therefore, be approved by others.

This was always assumed to be the case; therefore, the trend can be deceiving. By doing this, the true us—our identity—is removed. We need to maintain our resolve and integrity. Not because it's trendy, but because doing it is something everyone should do. Not every trend needs to fit with our individuality. We shall create our own signature style and fad to represent who we are.

We are creating a legacy of creativity and distinction. Many things are thrown at us by those around us. We must learn to select the people that are truly important to us and to sort out the people who will benefit us by seeking someone we can trust from those people. Avoid allowing those bad ideas to harm you.

Everyone desired a partner with whom to love and be loved. Relationships, however, are not always enjoyable; they are frequently exaggerated. If you are in a relationship, you must be willing to love, no matter how challenging it may be. When it comes to love, we frequently have expectations, but what we are dealing with is the exact opposite. We do not need to look for love; it is already inside us. The key is to be patient and wait for the proper person to arrive. Finding someone who is unlike us and can complete and fulfill us is preferable to finding someone who is precisely like us. Real love often shows up at the most unexpected times.

We must savor each moment, even though there are many things that irritate you and you are still struggling. We will always feel incomplete if we keep searching for it. Learn to be satisfied, whole, and joyful in every part of your life. We are fortunate in every aspect. The most important guideline is to be grateful for what we have.

Do not push things if it is not yet the right moment; if we do, we will later regret it. God's plan is for everyone, therefore we must wait patiently and not interfere.

We will learn to look at ourselves independently, without any anxieties, and understand that we don't have to prove anything to others but rather appreciate what life has to offer as we age, as we approach our late 20s. Every encounter we had along the road taught us something valuable, and this seasoned us to know how to handle situations properly and helped shape who we became.

Jhona Micah Novillos Esteban
Author, Phases of the Moon

Eyes, window of our soul

Something supposed to be colourful

Something actually make us full

Of mockery of tongues sharp and painful

They say harsh according to your how you are
wrapped

Not knowing what's inside as

God had provided a golden heart that can

loveA soul as pure as a dove

They say what he believed

So let their lips bleed

As long as God is beside you

You will be his child and beautiful creature

I am who you say I am

God's servant and child

Heir to God's kingdom

Blessed by God above

Cherry Beth Gabuyo
Author, The Gift of the Season

In a world full of voices of who should you be, this book offers an insightful message of embracing your peculiar self in the way how the Creator designed you to be- to be set-apart Christians. Sometimes we are pressured too much about how the world sets the standard of living that we feel like an outcast and cannot go with the flow. If you are feeling that way, it is perfectly fine

because this book will bring you to the realization about the most essential- living a life according to God's very purpose.

Remymar Anis

Pastor/Author, Isa Dalawa Tatlo ng Buhay ko, ang pang-apat ay tutuparin ko

The book **I am who you say I am** is one of a kind, it will give us a moment to look back on our past and to move on our lives. It will also remind us that we have to live according to our uniqueness, according to the gift our Almighty God has given us. One of the quotes the author had written and had struck me was, "Choose to do what is good than what you know right, for not all right is good but all good is right." This really applies to all and is true to everybody. This book will also guide us how to have a better version of us because of the practical formulas the author suggests in this book. Do you want to know what are those formula? Grab a copy of this book, read it, be inspired and be transformed.

Foreword

When I was young, I looked at myself negatively. I felt like a poor and struggling youth. All I knew was, life is difficult. Every day was too much to endure. During my high school and college years, I regularly attended the Holy Mass and nurtured my relationship with God. However, I felt that something was lacking. I could not grasp the real essence of my life and the role of God in my being. In 2012, I experienced a massive blow which made me abandon God. I felt that He does not love me. However, God rescued and brought me back to His loving arms. That moment became the start of my deeper relationship with Him. I started seeing my identity not according to my perception and the perception of other people, but according to what God says. One of my favorite stories in the Bible is the one where Jesus asks Peter "Who do you say I am?". Peter answered, "You are the Christ, the Son of the living God." Our life will matter on how we see and perceive God. Do you see God as a loving God? Do you see Him as a prosperous God? Do you see Him as a compassionate God? Again, Jesus is asking you, "Who do you say I am?" Reading the book **"I AM WHO YOU SAY I AM"** brought me back to my real identity in Christ. I should always move towards God. Many live according to worldly standards. But this book gives me a clearer perspective of my real identity. There is more to our physical being and material possession. We should live a life according to what God has called us to do. Reading this book allowed me to love my authentic and real self. Always go back to what God says about you. Beauty is more than your skin color. Beauty is more than your physical feature. Beauty is more than the clothes you wear. Real beauty is what God talks about you. Today start living a life according to God's purpose in your life and declare these every day, "Lord, I am yours. I am who You say I am." Congratulations Author Marjorie for coming up with this awe-inspiring book. Keep shining!

Jonas U. Dupo
Author & Motivational Speaker CEO & President, Elevate Motivational Center

About This Book

I am who You say I am is a short book written to give inspiration to the youth. It talks about how we subscribe to the set of standards imposed upon us by modern societies. This is a time when challenges are pressing, and the youth frequently find themselves trapped in microcosms of confusion. With all of these in consideration, this book seeks to provide answers to those who are searching, a map to those who are losing their path, a motivation to those who are having a hard time understanding the wisdom veiled in various things. It encourages a search for an identity; for it is only by knowing the "self" that we can move forward to the right destination.

This book has two parts that are divided into four chapters. The first part talks about *what* the world tells us to be, coupled with the things that make us feel lost and confused. The second part on the other hand, echoes spiritual guidance that carefully leads us to our *true identity* with the help of biblical verses. It emphasizes the paramount importance of shaping a good character. It influences our holistic view of *who we should be*.

This book has poetic parts. All the chapters are interrelated. The author advises the reader to abide by the sequence.

Enjoy the book!

Contents

Introduction

Matthew 16:15-16

15 He saith unto them, But whom say ye that I am? 16 And Simon Peter answered and said, Thou art the Christ, the Son of the living God.

In the middle of nowhere, I look around but could not see anything. Darkness surrounds me. At first, everything is filled with silence as though I am inside an empty room. I kept searching for someone; ended up finding nothing. My heart starts to beat faster. As I pace, I could not make anything out. The confusion that immersed me is blurring everything. Who am I? Why am I here? The voices in my mind resound in refrain. I ask myself, *"Why couldn't I see the answer? Why do I keep searching?"*

The finish line is a haze; I could not find it. If this is a forest, I think I am lost. If this is an ocean, I feel like I am drowning and continuously dragged into the bottom. I feel like I am thrown from a high place, and no one is waiting to catch me as I fall. Has anyone ever wanted to save me? All of a sudden, I feel weary. I take a rest for a while; compose myself. And as I begin to walk again, I hear voices-different voices uttering words I hardly understand. It's frustrating.

They keep on murmuring; they never stop. I can't find where they are coming from. They are hiding.

My heart want to stop beating and my mind want to escape for a while. I can't contain it anymore. My body is trembling and then tears started to fall from my eyes. But something inside me that wants to continue, an eagerness to fight. Undaunted, I decided to walk and gain strength to finish this race. The journey is not paved, I try not to stumble many times. Yet I couldn't see the finish line. Nonetheless, I keep pushing myself to stand up and start again.I feel delighted when I see a light from afar. I run as fast as I can. I hope this is the end of the darkness and I am free. However, another way paves before me. Many people are there, passing me by.I try to speak and catch their attention but nobody answers me. I wonder where I am. *I wonder who I am.*

All I remember are those voices that keep haunting me until now. Getting back to reality, I'm following them, seeking for help but everybody is on rush. I don't have any idea what is in the end of the path. I was confused where to go. Would I join them? Or would I turn the other way? Would I trust my instinct follow the way many have taken? How can I find the answer? What my heart truly says is I should make the difference. I try to chase them but a force seems to pull me back. So, I turn and walk alone in the other side. Now I am amazed. I see a light appear before me and it's so much brighter than anything I have ever seen. I am startled when Someone appear beside me. I feel relieved when He holds my hand. My heart is engulfed with unexplainable joy. As the journey continues, I notice that there is just one shadow and one pair of foot mark in the ground. He is carrying me during my hardest time. He is the one who keeps sending me courage. Memories come back and I am renewed. He asks me if I already know who I am. I answered I am Your child, that's who You say I am.

Yes, I am a child of God, that's how I win this battle.

Marjorie Tadeo Aglugub

Author

Part 1
Ultimately Lost-Child Of World

Faded Beauty

"You don't have to be somebody, you just need to be perfectly you".

"MAGIC MIRROR ON THE WALL, WHO IS THE FAIREST, ONE OF ALL." You probably know this line. A magic word or should I say magic spell, since these are the words of the evil queen in the Snow White and the Seven Dwarves, every time she wanted to affirm that she was the most beautiful among all. Unfortunately, she always failed to hear it. In our day-to-day lives, we take a moment to look into the mirror to see our faces, memorize every angle of it. Have you ever asked, "Who is the fairest one of them all?". Or you simply tell yourself you look pleasant. Or adorable. Or beautiful. We come to that moment when, we are so conscious of our looks.

We always want to look good in front of others. Beauty has a great impact in our lives. The fact is, everyone really wants to be beautiful. But what does being beautiful mean? How can we become beautiful? I deeply wonder. I remember when I was a child, I wanted to look exactly like the people I watched in television. I admired them a lot because of their beautiful faces perfect body figures. Sometimes I tried to imitate them, how they talk, move, their sense of style. The way the models walk on stage, I even tried to do it. All of us have experienced this stage.

For sure, many still do it until now. Many of us are wanting to be just like them-the icons of beauty we see on screen. I admit I was once like everybody too. I used to have those "W*hat if...*", *"I hope... "*, and *"I wish I could be just like them."* This is when insecurities attack us. While some of us are busy wanting to be just like our superstar idols, others try to join pageants to have the title "Beauty Queen". Some become so engrossed in putting make ups, invest in jewelries so they could look shining and shimmering.

Many of us are so desperate to make our faces and skin smooth that's why we try every remedy that could accomplish the job. We try trending beauty products, all the expensive yet popular brands. Not only that. Others also try new hairstyle or go to the gym to build some muscles. Sounds cool right? Do they get satisfaction after doing this? Do they gain happiness? I once experienced ordering beauty products online because it is a trend. I also tried applying on my skin them but didn't get the result I was expecting. I was so disappointed. I think that's the answer. Not all of us are satisfied and happy with the results. I have known some people who fell victim of this what we call beauty standards.

One time, a girl broke up with her boyfriend. He left her for someone he deemed more attractive. She was devastated. She cried a lot. Eventually she became desperate to try out different beauty products so she can turn into a swan. This girl was bullied because she's chubby. She ended up sacrificing her meals so she can lose weight. Someone made her inferior because she has pimples all over her face. She became too concerned. She wanted to find remedy to gain that smooth skin.

I think you are already aware of such scenes. Does it mean that when you're fat, don't have white and smooth skin and other good physical qualities, you can't be considered beautiful? That you can easily be dubbed as ugly? Is this what the society tries to point out today? That beauty can easily be defined? There are lots of people who lost their confidence and self-esteem because of how society defines beauty. They became broken, wounded and depressed because of harsh criticisms and judgments. I will not wonder why others reach the point where they become so obsessed of beauty and wanted to change their appearance. What does beauty really mean?

Do we really need to look like models, and beauty queens? Do we need to join beauty pageants, build muscles, wear shimmering jewelries, put some make up on, have a new hairstyle to be called beautiful? Don't get me wrong, I'm not against it nor am I judging anyone. Since we have different reasons and intentions why we wanted to do those things. Don't worry I have insecurities too and there are times when I struggled to get over them. But I just wanted to wake you up, make you realize the true meaning and essence of beauty. For I'm worried that you may be in a situation where you are lost and confuse because you are already consumed with this world and it's own definition of beauty. It is not bad to be beautiful. It is, however, wrong to try to be something or someone you're not. Just be yourself. Be your own version of beauty.

"MAGIC MIRROR ON THE WALL WHO IS THE FAIREST, ONE OF ALL". Did you ever notice the reflection in front of you in the mirror? Hey, I want to say you are the fairest of them all. Because you are beautiful in your own unique way. Don't ever forget that. You are beautiful in your own way.

Unsuccessful

"Everything has season, in the right time you will bloom just enjoy the process".

It was a sunny day and I felt a little bored. I decided to open my social media account and started scrolling. I came across some posts from close friends, relatives, batch mates and familiar people about their achievements in life, their careers, studies, travels and adventures. I felt a sudden heartache. I'm not sure but there's a little lump in my throat. My world stopped for a moment and I asked myself, what have I done all these years? Why do I feel so stuck? As if I did nothing. Why do I feel like I was left behind despite of all of those hard works and busy days.? Do I have to be jealous with the success of others? Does it help to be envious? I felt guilty, and depressed at the same time. Then I just decided to turn off my phone.

Have you ever been that situation? Have you ever gotten into a mood where you feel so empty and unproductive? Have you ever felt like the whole world is moving forward and you are left behind? There are lots of instances when this kind of feeling grips me. In surveys, it is always everyone's priority to have a career, to be on top of the class, to be financially capable, to be wealthy. Who wouldn't wish for that right? Everybody wants to be both intelligent and wealthy. If you add up these two, they seem to beperfect combination.

Why do we want to be intelligent? Does it guarantee us good career prospects? Of course, we should definitely have a good grade to be able to land in a good job, earn money and perhaps, be wealthy. We need good grades so good companies will hire us and we can have a source of income and provide for our families. There's nothing wrong with wanting to become intelligent and financially stable. But sometimes we put these into the wrong perspectives. Remember not to dig deeper into the concept of intelligence that you end up pressuring yourself. Don't be too hard on yourself. Each of us are given intelligence. Don't force it. It will come out naturally. What does our surroundings teach us about intelligence? If you have good grades, on top of the class, graduate with honors, land in a nice job, promoted to a higher position, you are intelligent. That is society. It defines almost every concept based on its selfish standards.

Money. Not everything is about money. While it does motivate us to work harder, making it the center of our lives does not make us as prosperous as we dream. Money buys you expensive things, takes you to beautiful places. It provides you comfortable life, lots of material things. That's why many people end up doing crimes to gain money.

Sometimes the success you see in others bother you. But for what are these? They serve as basis, something we could draw inspiration from. Some people, however, consider it a defining factor of who they are. They make it look like they are better than others because of what they have attained. But remember, success does not have one definite definition. Don't be fooled. I've noticed some people belittling the achievements and status of others. They seem to look down on vocational and non-board courses. They look down on farming and gardening. These do not define success. Again, don't be fooled.

We are engulfed in a lot of social constructs such as success lies in bachelor's degree, master's degree or doctorate degree. It is in riches and fame and beauty and perfection. But what about happiness? We toil so much for these so-called social constructs that we forget to laugh and live and love. We work so hard to please other people. Sometimes the reason why we push ourselves so hard is to conform. We try everything to fit into the definition of success, we forget our passion. We forget our talents. We abandon our principles.

Trying to be someone you're not is not at all, psychologically healthy. Do not strive for something just to please others. Do not be pressured by other's progress. Everybody has her/his own time to shine, you should wait for your spotlight. For the meantime, give your best shot. Enjoy every process, take it step by step. The fruit of hardwork and diligence is sweeter.

Work hard for everything you dream of. It's better to be slow but sure. We have our own journey. We don't need to compare ourselves to others. So, what should we do? Focus on ourself, don't be on hurry. Be patient in waiting. Pursue your own passion, make a name for yourself. I am telling you this so you won't be pressured. Don't mess with your world because of this feeling that you're being left behind. Just take some moment to look on yourself. There is happiness that money can't buy.

Out Of Trend

"Choose to do what is good than what you know right, for not all right is good but all good is right".

Tik tok, tik tok! I thought that was the sound of a clock but I was wrong for that is the newest trending app. I suddenly stopped when I heard a voice from my friend asking " Is this alright?" ,"Do I look good with this?", "Come on! Can you take a photo of me? I will just post it on my I.G please!" ,"Wait, can you fix it I think I look fat in this angle."

That is just a typical scene nowadays. Techy is the new name for those who are good in using technology or gadgets. Almost yearly, there is a new update in gadgets. And most people would stop on shops just to buy all of these even in expensive price. That's the trend. I remember one time; my friends and I went out for a meal in a fast food. After a long hour of waiting, our order was served. When we're about to eat, one of our friends stopped us by saying, "Wait I will just take picture. I will post it later." She told us that's the new trend, to engage and be active on social media, gain numbers of likes and reactions.

And if you are new to a place or have new stuff you should click on your camera and post it immediately.

Some tries to be a vlogger to beat for millions of followers and subscribers. Some are really worried without seeing the comment section, they are too bothered. That's the world our generation has been used to right now. Day by day our world continues to develop. With the technology today, distance do not matter. You can connect wherever you are. But wait there's more not just technology.

While others are busy with this social media, there are also those who are too engrossed in their OOTD's or Outfit of the Day. New styles of clothes are being introduced every day. Some people match their outfits with piercings too. Others love arts so much that they put tattoos all over their bodies. It's all about self-expression.

"Let's go to a party! Come on you need a break too. Do you want to join us? Let's s have some drinks. "It's okay to party, to unwind once in a while. But do you really need to drink too much until you're wasted? Do you really need to display your body? Some would take photos of themselves clad in a mini skirt, cleavage showing to gain lots and lots of reactions. While it is true that we can always wear what we want as a form of self-expression, too much exposure for the sake of popularity, I think isn't at all impressive. How we behave in social media should be coupled with utmost responsibility. If we wanted to showcase something we should be doing it for all the right perspective and intention.

You may say I am a bit of a judge. But I am not. Let's look into it and be awake. That's the truth. These trends, all that are happening right now aren't supposed to turn you around. Going with the flow is a choice. You won't be left behind simply because you refuse to subscribe to the trend. That's are the happenings of today and if you can't go with this flow, they will tell you out of trend. The way we dress, speak and act, the way we express who we are doesn't need to be compromised because of the thought that we might be left behind.

Sometimes barrier for understanding arises that we begin to fight one another. It is disappointing that even the words we speak are now turning foul. This is a natural scene in internet cafe where youths are busy playing this trend games. Wake up!

Do you need to be famous that bad, that you will risk your own identity just so you can go with the trend? Do you really need to resort to violent words, to offensive words to prove a point? Do you really have to prove a point? I remember this news about a 25-year-old teacher who got arrested for posting malicious and scandalous tweet. "I will give 50 million rewards to someone who can kill President Duterte". When asked why she did that, she answered that she only wanted to get attention. To the young people outthere, please be reminded on your accountability when using social media. You can't just post something without assuming responsibility.

What I'm trying to say is lot of people are really into this trend, they forget about responsibility. Others would reason out boredom. But do we need to seek attention? Social media nowadays is really taken for granted. Click here, share there. Even nonsense fights are being posted without accountability. Wrong actions will remain wrong even if many are doing it. So why would you do that too?

If you don't have lot of likes, followers, subscribers it's still okay. You don't need other's approval. You don't need to imitate other people's style and whatsoever. Even if you don't go with the flow, you can still be in trend. Even those famous people who have lot of fans are wishing for privacy. So why do you want that popularity? The fact is, you don't have to document all of these things because those uncaptured moments are the best and most treasured. Be you. Embrace you. Do what makes you, you. Don't just conform. Create an identity for you. A distinct, unique identity you will be known for.

Unworthy Loner

"Learn when to let go and when to hold on".

Let's talk about relationship.

Friends-close friends, best friend and *couples.* Wounded, would they still continue searching? Even if they are broken, will they still find ways to work things out? Who would not want to fall in love and be loved? That butterflies in your stomach, that joy you feel when you're hanging out with friends, it is unexplainable and priceless. But who are you when you're with them? *Are you the real you?*

A famous quotation says "Tell me who your friends are and I will tell you who you are." Who really are you? We are always reminded to be careful of the company we choose. One time I asked myself who am I? it took me hours and I have not yet arrived to an answer. This caused me to overthink too much that I end up sleep-deprived.

There are really moment when we don't even know ourselves. Having friends is great, having circle of friends is better. Having someone who will join you in everything, a support system, someone who will make you remember to laugh when you're in tears and most specially, someone who will give advice when your world is full of doubts and confusion. That really feels great. Others want a lot of friends, why? Because they believe the more, the merrier. It is cool to have more friends that's their motto.

I remember while we were having dinner in our dorm during my college, we have had some talks about friendship. My dormmate said, in the middle of our argument, "You are both different from each other. If you're a good friend, then she must be a true friend." But wait, is a good friend different from a true friend? She answered yes, it was different. True friends will tell things frankly while good friends will always protect you. If you're still confused and ask me how they differ, I am really wondering too.

Here it is, the wrong notion of this so-called friendship. People thought because your friends, you should be doing everything that there does. That's why when you don't join them, it's friendship over. Funny right? What if what they are doing is already wrong, would you still join them? Because if you don't you would probably end up a loner.

During my high school, there are times when a row of chair inside the classroom were vacant because a group of friends have talked with each other and decided to get absent. "All for one, one for all". Even in cutting classes, they have each other's back. When our teacher checked the attendance, all of them were not around. "In or out, are you in or out". Oops, that's not the lyrics of a song you probably thinking of. Instead. that was the line heard when someone wants to impose something on you. "So do you want to go with us?". This is very wrong!

Would you also believe that your friends will be your best enemies? Yeah, of course it is possible, for that long time you've been hanging out together, for sure you spilled all of your secrets to each other. And worst, friends are fond of doing unnecessary stuff. Some friends are into competition. If I ask you now, what kind of friendship do you have? Is your relationship healthy? Let's move on and dig deeper.

How about your status? Are you single, taken or loitering on the path of "it's complicated". Are you the Maria Clara of the group, where in all of your friends are really concerned because you remain to be alone while all of them are already into relationships.

If you feel like the reaction of your friends is too much, your parents are for sure more worrisome and are probably plotting to match you with someone since you don't have anyone yet. I thought this scene just happens during the early times.

Are you suddenly pressured because they bully you a lot for being single? So when a man tries to court you, you take the plunge and ends up with him. Or you try a dating app. Anything so you can finally get a relationship. Take it slowly. Do you need to be in a relationship because society is pushing you? That's a lame reason. And for those in relationship, they sometimes take it for granted because of wrong notions. The, prove your love to me by giving me your body is such a cliche, popular script of those boys who are trying to trick you. Where is the respect there? I'm sure that's not love but lust. Why is everybody in a hurry. Let's not be deceived of the world definition of love.

Is it necessary to maintain this status? This is why others engaged in premarital sex and end up bearing a child at a very young age. There are even times in social media when scandalous videos leaked. It's alarming. A lot of young people are being victimized. Some are way too young to be exposed to cybercrimes and cyberbullying.

Be very careful. If there are people who invite you to something you think isn't at all beneficial, refuse. You are allowed to say no. Do not get influenced. Instead, deepen your connection with God. Connect to people who are good for your emotional and spiritual growth. Do not let misuse of social media leads your destruction.

Learn to let go of those unreal people surrounding you. Create a stronger version of you.

Part 2
Renewing Soul-Child Of God

Simply Unique

Formula: Beautiful = Confident + Good Character

Bible verse:

Genesis 1:26-27

26 And God said, let us make man in our image, after our likeness: and let them have dominion over the fish of the sea, and over the fowl of the air, and over the cattle, and over all the earth, and over every creeping thing that creepeth upon the earth.27 So God created man in his own image, in the image of God created he him; male and female created he them.

Proverbs 31:30

"Favour is deceitful, and beauty is vain: but a woman that feareth the LORD, she shall be praised."

Are you also standing in front of mirror right now and your reflection is blurred? Your heart is heavy and you feel worthless, unaccepted, unappreciated. Your thought is full of doubts and insecurities strike you down. Little by little you are drowning, wounded and broken because of criticisms that keeps haunting you. Cheer up! You don't need to feel like that the whole time. Compose yourself, get back to where you begin.

How?

You need to eliminate the things that blocks you from seeing your reflection. Wipe up all those things that hinders you from seeing your true reflection. Yes, exactly that's what you need. You need to be reminded that we are created by God (Genesis 1:26-27). Yes, we are created in God's likeness and His own image so we don't have to be so worried about our looks. I believe God's creations are surely and hundred percent beautiful. Now stop doubting. Let's walk out from our room and put that smile again. Gain the confidence and be ourself. Be proud that we are made by God. We are perfectly beautiful and uncomparable. God created us uniquely, that's why we don't need to compare ourself to others.

He made every piece of us wonderful, a perfect design that will fit into us so don't try to change ourself. Other's opinion about our appearance is not important, especially if this will not give merit to us. If we feel broken because of our surroundings, we just have to seek God. He is always close to us and will heal us. We don't have to be in panic. Stay calm and be at peace. We shouldn't also focus on what we see in others. For they say everything that is seen on earth is deceiving. And what is here is just temporary. We don't have to fill ourself with the world definition of beauty. For what is more important is how God sees us.

Humans may be too ideal when it comes to appearance. Don't despair for God looks beyond physicality. For physical appearance will not last, it will fade soon. We undergo stages in life. We continue to grow and change is all around. Our faces will soon get old and will have wrinkles. Our body will change and deform but a good heart will always be good. After beauty is gone, the heart will remain. Physical appearance may trick us so we should really be careful. We should focus more in our inner beauty. Inner beauty is more beneficial. The bible reminds us to be simple and unique. We don't need to acquire all things. This is why physical appearance does not matter more than inner beauty. Don't try to be beautiful in front of others. Do everything to be beautiful inside and out in front of God. I mean we have to fear God and praise Him (Proverbs 31:30). For this world has high expectation, it is really tiring to do it all.

But God doesn't require all of this. What He wants us to do is to surrender our life to Him and walk with Him daily. Even though our heart sometimes is hidden with us, God knows what's inside it. You will become happy when you stop wanting someone else and start loving yourself by accepting who you are, what's in you. You will learn your value. your worth and you will know that you are incredible.

We must stop getting jealous, affected and paranoid. Instead, fill our heart with good qualities. If we worry so much, nothing will happen. So trust God always. Let us not be afraid to be who we are. If we let insecurities in, it will steal our value, peace, satisfaction, love and appreciation of our true self. It will lead us to wanting to someone else. Eliminate these insecurities and show kindness. Forgive people. Love unconditionally. Live in goodness that others may see God in us. Remember our actions reflect who we are. Let us be reminded that God's loves us for who we are. So we don't need to compare ourself to others because we don't have to prove anything to them. Our value comes from the creator and our worth will only be found in Him. Our value should be solely based on our good qualities, our character for we are children of God. It's really true that we glow differently if we are in Christ. Let our life be a reflection of Jesus and the Lord will be our confidence to face everything. If we're lacking confidence we must pray to God and He will give it to us. God wants us to be beautiful, of course. But giving too much time in working out our appearance is not really advisable for if this became the center of our attention, we will be unsatisfied.

In everything we do, we must have the good intentions. Let us not base our standard in others and start living in the standard of God.

Happily At Peace

Formula: Success = Contentment + Patience

Bible verse:

James 3:13, 17

13 Who is a wise man and endued with knowledge among you? let him shew out of a good conversation his works with meekness of wisdom.17 But the wisdom that is from above is first pure, then peaceable, gentle, and easy to be intreated, full of mercy and good fruits, without partiality, and without hypocrisy.

1 Timothy 6:10

For the love of money is the root of all evil: which while some coveted after, they have erred from the faith, and pierced themselves through with many sorrows.

Ecclesiastes 3:11 (KJV)

He hath made everything beautiful in his time: also he hath set the world in their heart, so that no man can find out the work that God maketh from the beginning to the end.

Are you in a race where you keep on running but couldn't reach the finish line? You feel tired yet not moving. You've done so many things but they're not enough. You're still stuck again while looking around you, you notice there achievements in life. You are surrounded with intelligence and wealth of people all around, while you, you feel unsatisfied. You view it like their lives are so fulfilled. And they are grateful because they have everything they want. Their big dreams and goals in life are perfect. But here you are, feeling uncapable, pressured and empty. So you keep on running and running, wanting to reach them too.

Look at yourself! You're forgetting something very important. If others are grateful, you are blessed. God is always there for you. You shouldn't feel bad about yourself. You are more than worthy. It's not because others keep on moving on top of their big dreams. It doesn't mean you are being left behind. The bible tells us that there is time for everything (Ecclesiastes 3:11). That's why we should patiently wait for our time. We shouldn't be on rush because Gods plan is much perfect than ours. Soon, in the right time with prayer and faith, we will be receiving those desire of our heart. If we didn't receive yet those things we keep on asking God, we shouldn't feel bad and disappointed. God doesn't give it yet because He is protecting and preparing us for better a purpose.

God answers prayers not by how we want them to be answered but by what is best for us. For as long as we keep on believing, God said He will not forsake us but will always guide us. His love is everlasting. We shouldn't fear for He will grant us all the capabilities and wisdom we need. Indeed, when the perfect time comes, we will have our own spotlight and God will let us shine so while waiting for it we should prepare ourself. We humans are created with different journey so let us not be bother to be pressured. Let us not compare ourselves with each other. Empower ourselves with positivity instead. God's blessing is abundance. Pursue only the things that we love most. Not only because they were achieved by others but because we want them too.

Education is seen in our behavior. We should be able to recognize what makes us better from the things that are not beneficial. For God keeps reminding us to be contented in what we have and stop worrying for He will provide. That's why we shouldn't focus on what we don't have. We should be contented and thankful for what is in us. Cherish it and enjoy everything.

It is not bad to gain the intelligence of the world, to be wealthy and to pursue our dreams. God wants His children to be successful, to be happy and fulfilled but we should know our limits too. For too much is bad. Let's look first on what the bible is telling us about loving money and how it will destroy us (1 Timothy 6:10). We shouldn't be blinded of the worlds definition of success. Don't let this become the center of our life for it will steal, corrupt and lead us to destruction. This might surely separate us from God. Loving the things in this world will make us lose our purpose. As they say, we cannot praise two masters at the same time. It is true that those things that steal our time and get our attention lead us to idolatry. They make us greedy. Someone told me that intelligence is not about how complex our mind is but how we spiritually grow. The application of all our learnings on the scripture is what intelligence means (James 3:13, 17). And the main purpose why God blessed us is to become a blessing to others, to share and help others through those we have received.

Let us avoid becoming greedy and envious of others. These will not grant us peace of mind. We will always feel lacking and wanting more. There are things that money and intelligence cannot give. So let us not be too busy gaining these two things to the point that our time to God will suffer. Earn wealth in heaven not in earth. Now let us start choosing what really matters. Find what God wants us to do, seek Him and pray that He will grant us the wisdom to do His will and remain in His ways. Stop those negative thoughts now and fix our eyes to God so whenever we feel this way again we will not be shaken. Don't chase things that are not meant for us. If it's truly for us God, will make a way. In pursuing everything we should put Him in priority. And ask always that He may give us a pure and clean heart so that we will have the good intentions. If we believe in God we can be more than what we want to be. We can't be successful without God. For true success comes from above, success that will lead us to eternal life. Blessings are coming, contentment is the key to a happy living. There is no greater wealth than having a peaceful mind.

Act In Goodness

Formula: Trendy = Offer yourself to God + Do good -Worldly habits

Bible verse:

1 John 2:15-17

15 Love not the world, neither the things that are in the world. If any man love the world, the love of the Father is not in him.16 For all that is in the world, the lust of the flesh, and the lust of the eyes, and the pride of life, is not of the Father, but is of the world.17 And the world passeth away, and the lust thereof: but he that doeth the will of God abideth forever.

Romans 12:1-2

1 I beseech you therefore, brethren, by the mercies of God, that ye present your bodies a living sacrifice, holy, acceptable unto God, which is your reasonable service.2 And be not conformed to this world: but be ye transformed by the renewing of your mind, that ye may prove what is that good, and acceptable, and perfect, will of God.

Ephesians 2:10

For we are his workmanship, created in Christ Jesus unto good works, which God hath before ordained that we should walk in them.

If you're standing in the middle of two paths where would you turn and walk into? Is it on the narrow road or the wide road one? Is it on where most people walk or you would rather walk alone? You may be confused right now and thinking if you will go with the flow. You wanted to try something new even if you aren't sure if it will be okay. Others keep on doing it that's why you follow their step.

Day by day we do a lot of activities-lot of tasks to complete, we keep ourself busy and occupied. But are all of these worthy? Are we doing it because it was acceptable to many? As our society continues to improve and developed, the things around us are also changing. We need to adopt and do some adjustment too. But take note, we should be sure that these changes and adaptation we are doing are good. As we're looking into the world, all of the trends, we should also learn to reflect. We are so blessed that God gave us the free will to do the things we want, choose right from wrong. This opportunity given to us should not be misused and abused. For the bible warns us, we, the children of God not to love the mundane things or even join the world (1 John 2:15-17). I mean those bad habits. Temptations are all around, our enemy is moving for us to be lost. That's why we should stand firm and be picky of the things we are following. Let us eliminate those bad influences. Don't waste our time doing things that are really unnecessary. Sometimes, because we feel the pleasure and we are at the comfort zone, we tend to continue to embrace the moment even its already harming us. These pleasures don't give the true happiness. They are just temporary. Just like the bible tells us, we will gain the whole world but if we lost our soul, it will be useless.

Some taught me that all of the things around us belong to the world but if we use it for the glory of God it will be worthy. This simply tells us not to conform with the world (Romans 12:1-2). You may please others, but do you reflect if God is happy in what we are doing? Time is moving let's talk to God and do the things that will please Him. For we are created to do good (Ephesians 2:10). Instead of beating the challenge of the world, why not engage ourselves in godly things like devoting our time to Him? Start building and improving our relationship with God. We should offer our life to God and not to the world. Join activities that will nourish our spiritual needs. Be active in church ministry and commit ourself in doing good to others.

Our body is the temple of God and the Holy Spirit dwells in us. We should take care of it and never destroy it. As a steward, we should make sure that this is in good condition. Build ourself, do not destroy it. If the world offers for us to go with the flow, follow others and be trendy, be widely known, God wants us to shield our characters, humble ourself and follow the good works. Just like what Jesus Christ set before us as an example. He came to serve not to be served.

Let us make Jesus known through our action. We should praise God in everything we do. We shouldn't imitate and follow the world. What we need is act in goodness and cast away evil. Avoid the things that will make us fall to sin. Stop being the follower of the world and start doing heavenly things for we don't need to be like everyone else. What we need is to offer ourself, holy and acceptable in God's eye. We should learn to control ourself and if we feel like the world is pulling us, wear God's word all over us so that we will not get lost and we will have the strength to fight against the enemy.

God gave us the Holy Spirit to help and guide us. Be transformed. Renew our soul. Read the bible. Meditate. Pray. Attend church always. Share the message and act in goodness. This is the real trend to be followed and nothing more. Don't be afraid to choose a different path from others for we don't have to be blinded by them. Instead, find a track that will bring us to peace. Let God be our guide in every path we are crossing so that our life will become easier.

Happiness is part of a mindset and it always depends on how we view and look at things. We have to learn not to acquire happiness from earthly things. Yes, we have the right to believe whatever we want to believe but not everything we believe is right. Whenever you don't understand the world, as everything else is becoming out of control, learn to close your eyes, take a deep breath and start a conversation with God. Remember that we are under His palm, holding us. We are called to be faithful and not to became famous. It will just destroy you if you keep holding on to that spotlight. Fame will soon crash but character will be forever. We have to do what God command us. Never be afraid of being different as long as you're obeying God's will.

We must avoid the companion of fool for what they bring us is harm. Instead of following the crowd, follow Jesus for He is the way, the truth and the life. He will bring us to the Father. Don't blend with darkness. Let us shine and stand out when it gets darker. Let's become fishermen who share the good deeds and the great message to others. Have faith and don't get stuck in the mundane ways. Be willing to change for the better. Reset our mind and soul, have a fresh and good vision and be planted in God's work. Let us prioritize God, spend more time with Him. If we renew ourself, we will see what God wants us to do and His ways for us. Life is a gift to cherish. Blessings are all around us, let's use this for God's glory. Let us not waste every opportunity to do good. If our roots is deep and in Christ, no need to fear. We are stronger and no one can defeat us. Even the world can't.

Realationship

Formula: Relationship = God centered + Building each other

Bible verse:

Ephesians 5:11

And have no fellowship with the unfruitful works of darkness, but rather reprove them.

Proverbs 13:20

He that walketh with wise men shall be wise: but a companion of fools shall be destroyed.

1 Corinthians 13:4-8

4 Love suffereth long, and is kind; love envieth not; love vaunteth not itself, is not puffed up,5 Doth not behave itself unseemly, seeketh not her own, is not easily provoked, thinketh no evil;6 Rejoiceth not in iniquity, but rejoiceth in the truth;7 Beareth all things, believeth all things, hopeth all things, endureth all things.8 Love never faileth: but whether there be prophecies, they shall fail; whether there be tongues, they shall cease; whether there be knowledge, it shall vanish away.

Are you afraid of losing someone? Did you ever fear losing yourself because of pleasing others? We feel isolated whenever we are alone that's why we always tend to seek others accompany. We put a lot of our effort to get along with people. We wish those moments we're with them never end. The world offers us different story of friendships and relationships. We have to risk our feelings just to be happy. But the bible teaches us the true standard on how to treat others and get along well. To threat everybody with good character, share with each other's burden. Let us be inspired by the story of David and Jonathan with their friendship, how they demonstrated it. It is important that we should build each other. Thus, we should find people who will empower us. It is more captivating to have friends who will lead us closer to God. A friend who will lift and remind us that God is always there. A friend who will make us a better person. One who will correct us when we are wrong and give us constructive feedback. We should avoid the people who blind us, hinder us to become the best version of ourselves. Let's be friend with those people who will stick to us in good times and bad times, who will motivate and help us improve our relationship with God. Let us be with people who will pull and save us from the dark, lead us the way back to light. Be surrounded with people who exude positivity and talk about dreams instead of gossiping. Seek people who will influence us to do good and will help us reflect the love of God. Let us be with people who know how to love unconditionally. That's the true meaning of friendship. We must avoid and let go of those people who will corrupt our characters, the one who will pull us to sin (Ephesians 5:11, Proverbs 13:20).

We don't need a lot of friends. What we need is a friend who is full of God's love is loyal and true to us. Many people are emotionally paralyzed because they intend to please and chase people. We don't need to please all of them. We just need to be what God wants us to be. I once read that we shouldn't love people too much so that if they leave, we will not be shaken. If we get along with other people, we should be real, no pretention. We must bring each other's true identity. We should bring each other to God. We should not harm each other. Treat one another well and grow in Christ together. It is good that we share our faith together. And if we are find love, let the bible guides us to the true meaning of love (1 Corinthians 13:4-8).

Contrary to what the world is teaching us, love does not cause suffering. Love always looks for happiness. Love is free from greed, envy and evil. It is full of kindness, equality, hope and truth. Love never gets tired.

We should find someone who will be a partner in ministry and serving God, one whom you can pray with. Someone who will show respect to us and will not force us to immorality. Remember that our body is the temple of God and Holy Spirit dwells in us. We must not let immorality takes us. The best relationship is manifested in mutual growth in the presence of God. We have to look not for a knight in shining armor but for one who is covered full with God's armor. Look for a God centered relationship bonded with love, loyalty and understanding that will give a delight to our heart. Such relationship will last forever. If we prioritize God always, every relationship will work well. Now if you feel unsuccessful with your relationship, remember that even others will leave you but God is always there for you. Prayer moves the world. It is a very powerful weapon.

Let's pray to find the best relationship. Just because you don't see anything happening in your relationship with others doesn't mean God is not working. He is working. God's timing isn't our timing. He may not be working according to our plan but He is working for our best. Let us trust Him for God is always in control. Let us stop looking for love in the wrong place. We should seek love from the source of everything, our God for He first loved us. We must first fall in love with Him. The missing piece of our heart is sometimes not filled by our fellow human but by God. Let God fill all the emptiness in our heart. Give it all to Him. Embrace God's presence in our life and we will know that He is enough.

We don't have to be in hurry to get into a relationship. Wait patiently for God has been saving us for a better love story. So for now, we must put all the love to God. Give love to ourself too so that we will spread it to others. We need to be selfless first before we learn to love. I mean, give and surrender yourself to God first, for in Him there is no pain but joy. A relationship with God is the best relationship.

YOU DONT HAVE TO BE SOMEBODY YOU JUST NEED TO BE PERFECTLY YOU.
FOR EVERYTHING HAS A REASON IN THE RIGHT TIME YOU WILL BLOOM, JUST ENJOY THE PROCESS.
JUST CHOOSE TO DO WHAT IS GOOD THAN WHAT YOU KNOW RIGHT FOR NOT ALL RIGHT IS GOOD BUT ALL GOOD IS RIGHT.
AND LEARN TO LET GO AND WHEN TO HOLD ON....
I AM WHO YOU SAY I AM
= CONFIDENT + GOOD CHARACTER + CONTENMENT + PATIENCE + OFFER YOURSELF TO GOD + DO GOOD -WORDLY HABITS + GODCENTERED + BUILDING EACH OTHER
inspired by: abstract artist

Conclusion: Unclothe Identity

1 Corinthians 3:16

Know ye not that ye are the temple of God, and that the Spirit of God dwelleth in you?

There is a moment when we don't know who we are. We try to search for the answers but what is in front of us seems different. We get so disappointed when we don't find the answers. Because we are so desperate, we tend to make shortcuts but end up broken and in pain. We start to doubt as confusion attacks us. There is this voice echoing over our ears just like what I illustrated in the introduction of this book. This voice sometimes shouts the criticisms the world throws on us.

We are so afraid to face the truth that's why we tend to believe what others tell us. Sometimes we rely on what we see. And that's how we get lost. It is the time when we are filled with the world that our emotions eat us. We are easily taken by the wave of it. What we embrace is the invite of the world and this becomes the center of our attention. We wear a mask that hide our true identity and become victim of destruction. We become too focuses on our surroundings and too busy with a lot of things that we forget the important ones. Most specially, we forget who we are. Maybe you are asking now: How will I discover the real me? The first step is to connect to the source of everything. Let God enter your life. Accept and embrace His love and grace.

We should give everything to Him for only He is able to help us. He will fix every piece of us. If we surrender our life to Him we will be lightened up. As we accept the salvation from God, we become transformed and renewed. we become a new creation. God chooses us and we are His children. Upon receiving His grace with faith, we should act. Give up those bad habits and evil works. We must break the chain that holds us, enslaves us. At first it will be difficult and painful because we are used to it. But if we focus and put our heart in eliminating these things, we will find something different-the delight and peacefulness of our soul.

We are created to do good things and follow Christ. We may have different journeys but we have one purpose: to praise God. If we think we are not doing the same thing like most people is doing thus we are left behind, we are not. We have to continue choosing what is righteous even if we may differ from others in a lot of things. We may gain the whole world but if we lose our soul, it is useless. For we become nothing.

Let us choose to enter the narrow way for the wide and broad way leads to destruction. Don't trust ourself. Trust in God for He knows what is best for us. We should be directed by Him. Put God in everything we are doing and we will not be lost. Do not be afraid for God continually uses instruments for us to be able to conquer everything.

You already read in the first chapter of this book about worldly standard and what it tells us to be. That to be beautiful we have to acquire and maintain good physical appearance, to be successful we have to gain the things in this world, to be in trend we have to follow others and go with the flow, to have good relationship we have to please everyone. But in second chapter we found out with the help of the bible, God wants us to know that real beauty comes within. It is in our good character. We should not focus on wealth and wisdom for these will be ruined by time. Instead focus on earning treasures in heaven, real success is gained with contentment and peacefulness in heart. We should not conform to the world. We should guard our heart and actions, for the real trend is doing godly things.

Lastly, true relationship is the one that puts God in the center. Thus, we must filter what we hear around us and stop absorbing words that will corrupt our good character. We must believe and have faith. We are the temple of God and the Spirit dwells in us (1 Corinthians 3:16), so we should protect ourself and make sure not to put it in sin. We have to be a good steward. Everyone should be willing and open to know the real meaning and essence of these things.

We must offer ourself holy and acceptable in front of God. Fill ourself with the Holy Spirit and wear the armor. It is the word of God, the truth that will set us free.

Do not get tired of doing good. In everything we do, we should do it for God. We should not live within other's standards. If we want change, change for ourselves and not for others. A change that is worthy and will make as grow spiritually. If before we became child of the world, we are now the child of God. We should not let the world win against us. Let us not go back to what we are doing in the past, rather move forward and shine. We must be the light in the darkness to shine for others and pull them closer to God too.

We have our own identity. We are different. We should stop imitating what is not good. If we nourish ourselves spiritually, there is no reason to feel lacking and unfulfilled. There is no room for negativity in all the children of God. We don't need money, intelligence, power, fame, and beauty. What we need is Jesus. We should remain faithful through the years for He is forever faithful to us. Our life may not seem perfect but we have perfect God who will lead us with this imperfect life with unfailing strength, incredible wisdom and infinite love.

We shouldn't reason that we are not perfect. We should seek perfection by connecting to Him for He is good and the most powerful. And the most important possession we should is our spiritual life.

We should guard our heart and be transformed to have the inner piece. The key to know yourself when you have already forgotten it is to seek God first. God is enough for us. we should entrust everything to Him, live by what the scripture tells us. We should keep our faith, continue doing God's will and we will see our true worth and we know who we really are.

About the Author

Please share your experience on how this book made an impact to you. How it helps, encourage, and blessed you?

Connect to **Marjorie Aglugub**,

Email: *Marjorieaglugub.MA@gmail.com*

Facebook: **Marjorie Aglugub**

Instagram: ***@limyeongwoo***

FB Pages: **"God's Artwork"** & **"Worth-dy"**

www.ingramcontent.com/pod-product-compliance
Lightning Source LLC
LaVergne TN
LVHW041751190726
843493LV00008B/2564